Authentic Christianity 101

Robert L. Dickie

EVANGELICAL PRESS

EVANGELICAL PRESS
Faverdale North, Darlington, DL3 0PH, England

e-mail: sales@evangelicalpress.org

Evangelical Press USA
P. O. Box 825, Webster, New York 14580, USA

e-mail: usa.sales@evangelicalpress.org

web: http://www.epbooks.org

First published 2007
Second impression 2009

British Library Cataloguing in Publication Data available

ISBN-13   978-0-85234-672-3   ISBN 0-85234-672-7

Printed and bound by Penny Print : (0191) 461 1111

Contents

	Page
Introduction	5
The existence of God	8
The nature of God	23
The gift of God	33
The promise of God	37
Conclusion	41
Notes	46
Scripture index	48

Introduction

'For God so loved the world, that he gave his only begotten Son,
that whosoever believeth in him should not perish,
but have everlasting life'
(John 3:16).

This verse in John 3:16 is perhaps the most well-known verse in the whole Bible. John's Gospel is the last of the four Gospels that were written on the life of Jesus. The word gospel means 'good news' and is from the Greek word *euangelion*, ευανγγελιον. The Bible is a collection of sixty-six books made up of two Testaments, the Old and the New. There are thirty-nine books in the Old Testament and twenty-seven books in the New Testament. All sixty-six books of the Bible, from Genesis to Revelation, are about one great theme — Jesus Christ. The word 'Bible' is from the Greek word *biblia*, βιβλια, and means books. The word 'Scripture' is from the Latin word *Scriptura* and means sacred writings.

The Apostles' Creed

Over the centuries, Christians have often recited the early Christian doctrinal statement known as the Apostles' Creed. The Apostles' Creed was written around AD 140 and is the oldest of all the great creeds of the Christian Church. This brief statement encapsulates the major points of the Christian faith.

When a person attends a Christian church and they hear the Apostles' Creed recited, they will have a good understanding of the major points of Christianity. The creed simply states:

I believe in God, the Father Almighty, the Creator of heaven and earth, and in Jesus Christ, His only Son, our Lord: Who was conceived of the Holy Spirit, born of the Virgin Mary, suffered under Pontius Pilate, was crucified, dead, and was buried. He descended into Hades. The third day He arose again from the dead. He ascended into heaven and sits at the right hand of God the Father Almighty, from thence He shall come to judge the living and the dead. I believe in the Holy Spirit, the holy Christian church, the communion of Saints, the forgiveness of sins, the resurrection of the body, and life everlasting. Amen.

Just as the Apostles' Creed gives us a good summary of the contents of the Christian faith, so, too, John 3:16 gives us a concise summary of the gospel of God's grace. If a person can understand the meaning of John 3:16: 'For God so loved the world, that he gave his only begotten Son, that whosoever believeth in him should not perish, but have everlasting life,' he will have a good understanding of how a person can be prepared for heaven.

In the first chapter of John's Gospel, we have the secret to the origin of all of life. 'In the beginning was the Word, and the Word was with God, and the Word was God. The same was in the beginning with God. All things were made by him; and without him was not any thing made that was made. In him was life; and the life was the light of men' (John 1:1-4). This is very similar to the first few verses of Genesis chapter one where we read, 'In the beginning God created the heaven and the earth' (Genesis 1:1). The Bible tells us that the origin of all life began with the work of God in creation. Man did not happen by chance or by evolution. God not only gave man life, but he also gave each man a soul. Because God made man in his image (with the ability to know right and wrong, to be moral, and to be creative), man has value and significance. Therefore, all men are important. This is why we take the time to consider the Christian message, because all people everywhere need to know how to prepare for death and the life to come.

The person who is described as the Word in John chapter one is the Lord Jesus Christ. We know this because of verse 14 which says, 'And the Word was made flesh, and dwelt among us, and we beheld his glory.' Jesus is the one that God sent to be the Savior of the world. In John chapter three, Jesus gives us a concise summary of what his mission and message were all about. We are going to talk about that message in this booklet. What we have in this brief text of John 3:16 is what I call 'Authentic Christianity 101'. These are the basic and elementary facts of what one must know and believe in order to be a Christian.

In John 3:16 we see that there are four things that are made clear to us about the God of the Bible. We will now consider the four truths that this great verse in John's Gospel shares with us.

1. The existence of God
2. The nature of God
3. The gift of God
4. The promise of God

All four of these great facts make up what are considered the basics of the Christian faith.

The existence of God

*'**For God** so loved the world, that he gave his only begotten Son,*
that whosoever believeth in him should not perish,
but have everlasting life.'

John 3:16 simply begins with this phrase, *'For God...'* Jesus
is the one who is speaking these words. He is assuming that
those who heard him speak believed in God. In fact, Jesus
not only assumes this, he makes this declaration without any
apology or qualification. Similarly, the Bible does not argue
for the existence of God; the Bible just assumes belief in God.
Psalm 14:1 says, 'The fool hath said in his heart, There is no
God.' Romans chapter one claims that everyone knows of
God's existence. Paul writes in that letter that all have an inner
understanding of God. This inner, or what some have called an
'innate' understanding of God, was given to everyone at birth.
People may try to deny this, but by nature, everyone really
knows in their heart that there is a God. Paul states, 'Because
that which may be known of God is manifest in them; for God
hath shewed it unto them. For the invisible things of him from
the creation of the world are clearly seen, being understood by
the things that are made, even his eternal power and Godhead;
so that they are without excuse' (Romans 1:19-20).

The question that we all have in light of this assumption of
God's existence is simply, 'What is God like?' The theologians
who wrote the famous *Shorter Catechism* give us a concise
statement in answer to that question: 'What is God? God is

a Spirit, infinite, eternal, and unchangeable, in his being, wisdom, power, holiness, justice, goodness, and truth.'[1]

Although the Bible assumes the existence of God, is there any evidence that supports the belief in the existence of a divine Being?

The classical arguments for the existence of God

In the study of theology, there are what have been called the *classical arguments* for the existence of God.

1. The *Universal Belief Argument* in the existence of God. This simply reminds us that on every continent and in every land, men all over the world have a basic understanding and belief that there must be a god. There simply is no land anywhere where all the inhabitants are atheists. Belief in God is a universal fact that no one can deny.

2. The *Cosmological Argument* or the argument from cause to effect. This is a universal truth observed by all men at all times. It simply reminds us that for every effect, there was something that caused that effect. Nothing ever happens without a cause. William Evans, a Christian theologian, defines the cosmological argument in this fashion: 'When we see a thing, we naturally ask for the cause of that thing. We see this world in which we live, and ask how it came to be. Is it self-originating, or is the cause of its being outside of itself? Is its cause finite or infinite?'[2]

3. The *Teleological Argument* from design and order which shows a purpose for creation. If we see a watch, we assume there was a watchmaker. On one winter night a few years ago, I saw this beautiful ice sculpture. It was a heart encapsulated

inside this very intricately designed cabinet of ice. Did I think to myself, 'Oh I bet that ice carving just formed in the skies and fell here without breaking and mashing, and it is now here for all of us to marvel at its beauty and amazing artistry.' No. I concluded someone put a lot of time into that work of art and how lovely it is to see the work of someone's skill and labors. Just as the ice sculpture had a designer, so, too, all of life teaches us that when we see something beautiful or complex it did not just happen by chance or accident. When we see design and order, it is our understanding that an intelligent designer has been at work. Norman Geisler, a writer who has written extensively on why the Bible is to be trusted and accepted as the Word of God, spoke on this very issue of intelligent design. He made this observation: 'If you came into the kitchen and saw the Alphabet cereal spilled on the table, and it spelled out your name and address, would you think the cat knocked the cereal box over?[3]

4. The *Ontological Argument* or the argument from Being, which means the very idea of God presupposes his existence. If there was not a God, why is it that men everywhere have such a lofty and wonderful idea that he exists?

5. The *Anthropological Argument*, also known as the moral argument. We argue that since man has a moral nature and a capacity to know right from wrong, this presupposes that God created man in his likeness.

6. The *Argument from Congruity*. This argues from the idea that the concept of God fits all of the facts that we have about ourselves and our world.

7. The *Argument from Scripture*. The Scriptures of the Old and New Testaments in the Judeo-Christian faith teach us that there is a God. These Scriptures are the authority that we stand

upon. It is important to remember that to disprove that there is a God, one would have to be able to prove that the Scriptures are not true and are not the inspired Word of the true and living God. What I am saying here is that that has never been done.

No one has ever been able to refute or to disprove that the Bible is the Word of God. I came across a poem many years ago that reminds us of how the Bible is able to withstand all the silly and futile attacks on its integrity and reliability.

The Anvil of God's Word

Last eve I passed beside a blacksmith's door,
And heard the anvil ring the vesper chime.
And looking in I saw upon the floor,
Old hammers worn with beating years of time.

'How many anvils have you had?' said I,
'To wear and batter all these hammers so?'
'Just one' said he, and then with twinkling eye,
'The anvil wears the hammers out you know.'

And so, thought I, the anvil of God's Word,
For ages skeptic blows have beat upon.
And though the noise of falling blows was heard.
The anvil is unharmed. The skeptics gone.

Author unknown

These classical arguments cannot prove that God does, in fact, exist. But taken together as a body of evidence, they do produce some very powerful and convincing facts that help lead us to conclude that there must be a God. These seven classical arguments for the existence of God provide a solid and logical basis for belief in a Supreme Being. Weighing all of this together we ask ourselves, 'Is it logical that man came from nothing and is here by pure chance?' We can answer 'Yes' to that question when we see the parts of an automobile produce and assemble themselves into a finished car without the help or aid of man. We can answer 'Yes' to the question when we see a jet airplane assemble itself from the debris in a junk yard and fly off by itself into the sunset. We can answer 'Yes' to this when we see a bridge build itself across some vast canyon without any engineers or human laborers. When these things happen by themselves, we can then conclude on the basis of logic that man could have evolved by chance. This is why these arguments for the existence of God are so helpful. They produce a solid foundation of logical reasons why the belief in God is not a mere leap of faith into the dark.

We must also remember that while we cannot argue a person into becoming a Christian, we can share facts and evidences that will be a great help to those who are already Christians. These evidences are often used to strengthen their faith. Those who are not Christians may have their questions and doubts answered, but ultimately they need the work of the Holy Spirit to convince them of their need of Christ and to enable them to repent and to believe in the gospel of Christ.

If we assume there is a God, the next question that follows is: 'Who is this God?' There are many different religions claiming to know and to represent the true and living God. These religions cannot all be true. So how do we know which faith is speaking the truth? I believe the answer is to examine the Scriptures of these various world religions. Jesus was once approached by some of his critics who asked, 'By what authority doest thou these things? And who gave thee this authority?' (Matthew 21:23). That was one of the most important questions a person could ask. The authority of any religion must ultimately stand on the Scriptures that they believe to be true. Therefore, I believe that the most effective way to discover who has the truth is by examining the various Scriptures that the different religions follow.

Five major world views

There are five major world views that claim to give us knowledge about God: either his existence or his non-existence.

1. *Islam*: held by those who believe in Allah and in the book called the Koran.

2. *Eastern Pantheism*: for those who believe in reincarnation and the gods of the East (Hinduism and Buddhism). Hindus follow the writings called the Vedas, Upanishads and the Bhagavad-Gita. Buddhists follow the Mahavastu ('Great Story', a chaotic collection covering the Buddha's life story), the Jataka Tales (550 stories of the former lives of the Buddha), the Tripataka ('Three Baskets'), and the Tantras (as recorded in Tibetan Buddhism).

3. *Judaism*: held by those who worship Jehovah but reject Jesus as the true Messiah. Adherents to Judaism follow the Scriptures of the Old Testament.

4. *Naturalism*: for those who are Communists, atheists and agnostics. These people do not follow any scriptures but are devout followers of various writings such as the *Communist Manifesto* by Karl Marx and Frederick Engels written in 1848, the *Humanist Manifesto*, and other secular philosophies.

5. *Christian Theism*: held by those who worship and follow Jesus Christ. Christians follow the teachings of the Bible that include the Old and New Testament.

This may be confusing for many when they are trying to find out what is truth. How can we really know, when there are so many different faiths out there claiming to be true? I believe that the Christian faith alone gives the most satisfying

and defendable answers as to the existence of God. I believe
in God because the Bible tells me that he exists. My belief in
God is dependent on the testimony of Scripture. The Christian
Scriptures can be examined and tested, and they alone are
unique from all other religious books. We find overwhelming
evidence to prove the truth claims of the Word of God.

Over the years, I have found great joy in presenting the
gospel message. I welcome questions to my faith. In fact, I
believe that the Christian faith alone can stand up to the many
questions and scrutiny of those who are seeking the truth.
There are five ways that I demonstrate that the Bible is the
Word of God:

1. Prophetically
2. Historically
3. Scientifically
4. Morally
5. Dynamically

These five areas of study, when taken together, form a
powerful argument for the reliability of Scripture and therefore
for the existence of God. Let me give a brief summary of what
each of these points says to us.

First, we know that there are over 2,000 prophecies in the
Bible. There are 333 prophecies concerning the coming of the
Messiah alone. Jesus Christ fulfilled them all. As we study the
Bible, we have never found that any of these prophecies have
ever been wrong. Not even once! This reminds us of what
the apostle Paul wrote to Timothy: 'All scripture is given by
inspiration of God, and is profitable for doctrine, for reproof,
for correction, for instruction in righteousness: That the man of
God may be perfect, thoroughly furnished unto all good works'
(2 Timothy 3:16-17). In the Koran there is only one prophecy
to validate the truth claims of that religion. Hear what one
scholar had to say about prophecies in the Eastern religions:

'In all the writings of Buddha, Confucius, and Lao-tse, you will not find a single example of predicted prophecy. In the Koran (the writings of Muhammad), there is one instance of a specific prophecy — a self-fulfilling prophecy that he, Muhammad himself, would return to Mecca. Quite different from the prophecies of Jesus who said that He would return from the grave. One is easily fulfilled, and the other is impossible to any human being.'[4]

One expert on Bible prophecy made this comment:

Unique among all books ever written, the Bible accurately foretells specific events in detail — many years, sometimes centuries, before they occur. Approximately 2,500 prophecies appear in the pages of the Bible, about 2,000 of which already have been fulfilled to the letter — no errors. (The remaining 500 or so reach into the future and may be seen unfolding as days go by.) Since the probability for any one of these prophecies having been fulfilled by chance averages less than one in ten (figured very conservatively), and since the prophecies are for the most part independent of one another, the odds for all these prophecies having been fulfilled by chance without error is less than one in 10^{2000} (that is 1 with 2000 zeros written after it)![5]

Here are some of the many Messianic prophecies that are found in the Old Testament and that were fulfilled by Jesus Christ.

Old Testament prophecy	New Testament fulfilment
1. Isaiah 9:6-7; born as a human male	Luke 2:7
2. Genesis 3:15, born of a woman	Luke 2:4-11; Galatians 4:4; Matthew 1:20
3. Isaiah 7:14, born of a virgin	Matthew 1:18, 23

Old Testament prophecy	New Testament fulfilment
4. Isaiah 7:14, named Immanuel	Matthew 1:23
5. Genesis 17:19; Numbers 24:17, from Abraham, Isaac and Jacob	Luke 3:34; Matthew 1:2
6. Genesis 49:10, from the Tribe of Judah	Luke 3:23,33
7. Isaiah 11:1-5,10, from the house of Jesse	Romans 15:12; Matthew 1:1-2, 5-6, 16
8. Isaiah 16:5, from the house of David	Matthew 1:1-2, 6, 16
9. Micah 5:2, born in Bethlehem	Matthew 2:1-6; Luke 2:1-20
10. Jeremiah 31:15, massacre of infants	Matthew 2:16-18
11. Isaiah 9:1-2, from Nazareth	Matthew 2:22-23; Matthew 4:13-16
12. Isaiah 9:1-2, from Capernaum (the region of Zebulun and Naphtali)	Matthew 4:15-16
13. Hosea 11:1; Numbers 24:8, come out of Egypt	Matthew 2:14-15
14. Isaiah 49:23, kings would bow to him	Matthew 2:11
15. Psalm 72:10, given gifts	Matthew 2:1,11
16. Leviticus 12:1-4, lives 33 years, and has a 3.5-year ministry	Luke 3:23
17. Malachi 3:1, messenger prepares the way for him	Matthew 11:10

Old Testament prophecy	New Testament fulfilment
18. Isaiah 40:3, another prophet would announce him	Matthew 3:1-3
19. Isaiah 35:5-6, Isaiah 29:18, miraculous healings	Matthew 9:35; Luke 7:20-22; Matthew 11:5
20. Isaiah 61:1-2, deliver spiritual captives, the poor hear the gospel	Luke 4:16-21; Matthew 11:5
21. Isaiah 53:1,3, Psalm 118:22, despised and rejected	Matthew 26:3-4; John 12:37-43
22. Psalm 69:4; Isaiah 49:7, hated without cause	John 7:48-49; John 15:24-25
23. Psalm 118:22, rejected by rulers	Matthew 21:42; John 7:48-49
24. Psalm 69:8, rejected by his brothers	Mark 3:20-21; John 7:1-5
25. Psalm 8:2, children would praise him	Matthew 21:16
26. Psalm 78:2, the Messiah would teach in parables	Matthew 13:35

These are just a few of the 333 prophecies that Jesus fulfilled in his life and ministry. The likelihood of any man being able to do this — be it by chance or by accident or coincidence — is completely unimaginable. It has been stated that the probability of any fifty of these prophecies being precisely fulfilled by any one individual is 11 sextillion 250 quintillion to one. When written out, this figure would look like this:
11,250,000,000,000,000,000,000:1.

Second, we consider the historical or archaeological evidence for the Bible. The fact remains clear that there has never been one point, not one historical fact in the Bible, that has ever been proven wrong based on the evidence of archaeological findings. As one writer has said: 'The significant point is that when sufficient factual information becomes known, and is properly interpreted, it confirms the biblical record.'[6] A noted archaeologist, Ira Price, after considering the overwhelming archaeological and historical evidence for the Bible said, 'These records, chiseled in adamantine volumes, stamped in perishable clay, painted in the darkness of the tombs, or cut on the mountain side, bring impartial, unimpeachable, and conclusive proof of the veracity of the Old Testament.'[7]

The *third* point teaches us that the Bible is scientifically accurate everywhere it speaks. We know the Bible is not a book of science. But since it is the Word of God, and since we believe that it was written by divine inspiration, we believe that where it speaks of scientific matters, it is accurate and correct. Dr Mark Eastman and Chuck Missler, a computer specialist, wrote in their book, *The Creator Beyond Time and Space*, '... when the biblical text is carefully examined, the reader will quickly discover an uncanny scientific accuracy unparalled by any document of antiquity... In virtually all ancient religious documents, it is common to find scientific inaccurate myths about the nature of the universe and the life forms on planet earth... However ... throughout the Bible we find scientifically accurate concepts about the physical universe that were not "discovered" by modern scientists until very recent times.'[8] Over the years I have enjoyed sharing with students some of the absurd theories that various cultures had concerning creation. It is important to understand that when Moses wrote about creation, his statements were a direct contradiction to all the known and accepted views of his day. For example, consider the following points:

- The ancient Egyptians thought the earth was hatched from a winged egg which flew around in space until the process of mitosis was complete. Yet Moses wrote, 'In the beginning God created the heaven and the earth' (Genesis 1:1).
- The ancient Egyptians thought men were originally hatched from white worms that lived along the banks of the Nile River. Yet Moses wrote in the Bible, 'The Lord God formed man out of the dust of the ground' (Genesis 2:7).
- The ancient Babylonians thought that the god Marduk killed a great monster called Tiamat and flattened out her body to make the earth. They also believed that wherever this god Marduk spat, men would spring up; and wherever the men would spit, women would spring up. Jesus Christ referred to Daniel as a great prophet, and in Ezekiel 14:14 Daniel is called righteous. There is not a trace of this Babylonian nonsense in the book that Daniel wrote in the Old Testament.
- Moses, who wrote the first five books of the Old Testament, knew that the oceans had one common floor. 'And God said, Let the waters under the heaven be gathered together unto one place…' (Genesis 1:9). The Hebrew word for place is *Magom* which means bed. The only sea Moses probably knew about was the Mediterranean and possibly the Atlantic Ocean. And yet, it wasn't until centuries later that all seven seas were found to have one floor or one ocean bed.
- Job, who wrote the oldest book in the Bible, said, 'He stretcheth out the north over the empty place and hangeth the earth upon nothing' (Job 26:7). When Job wrote this, the various world cultures had their own ideas as to how the earth was suspended in space. The Egyptians believed the earth was flat and was supported by five pillars. The Greeks believed the earth was supported on the shoulders

of a giant god named Atlas. The Hindus of India believed the earth was flat and balanced on the back of a giant elephant which was standing on an immense turtle, which was swimming in a great cosmic sea.

While the Bible is not a science book, it is fair to say that the Bible is accurate when it speaks of matters that deal with science.

The *fourth* pillar of proof for the Bible's reliability is found in the study of morality. The Bible gives the human race the highest standards of decency and morality that have ever been known to man. Virtually all great civilizations build upon the timeless principles of the Ten Commandments. We might also add that there has never been a more sublime and more practical statement of how to live than the one Jesus gave us when he said, 'Therefore all things whatsoever ye would that men should do to you, do ye even so to them: for this is the law and the prophets' (Matthew 7:12). This statement by Jesus has been called 'The Golden Rule'. We simply state it in this way: 'Do unto others as you would have them do unto you.' The Ten Commandments are the basis of judicial law worldwide. And the teachings of Christ in the New Testament are without parallel anywhere in the world.

Finally, the *fifth* area we use to prove the trustworthiness of the Bible is what I call the dynamic impact that the Bible has on the lives of those who read it. History is filled with countless testimonies of those who have had their lives changed by the message of the Christian faith. One student made these observations on the dynamic impact the Bible has had on Western civilization:

- the founding and development of modern science and law;
- the founding and development of medicine and health care, involving the first establishing of hospitals;

- modern education, including the founding of nearly all major American universities, such as Princeton, Harvard, Yale and Dartmouth;
- providing a logical basis through absolute values for the advance of ethics in general, including sexual morality, which in our time alone has saved millions of lives;
- protecting the dignity of marriage and family life, which greatly contributes to the stabilization of society;
- instituting political freedom and human rights generally, including the abolition of slavery and protection of the unborn, infants, children and women;
- inspiring major contributions to the best in art, literature, music and architecture;
- undergirding vast humanitarian endeavors globally, supporting the dignity of labor and economic reform.[9]

British author Os Guinness also understood the amazing impact that the Christian faith has had on mankind. His comments in his book *The Long Journey Home* should remind all of us that this would be a very different world if the message of Christ were missing from it. Guinness writes:

> *The fact is that almost all great reforms in Western history —*
> *including the banning of infanticide, the abolition of slavery,*
> *the rise of women's movement, and progress in civil rights —*
> *have been inspired by faith and led by people of faith. Yet faith*
> *itself is commonly dismissed as reactionary.*
>
> *Still another fact is that secular ideologies, not religion, proved*
> *responsible in the last century for the Holocaust, the Gulag, and*
> *the killing fields. And that religion, not secular philosophies, was*
> *influential in providing the world wide thrust for freedom and*
> *democracy in the last several decades.[10]*

Four great men who were overwhelmed by the evidence for the resurrection of Christ

Many years ago there were two gentlemen from England who attempted to disprove the Bible. They were Lord Lyttleton and Gilbert West. Lyttleton was a member of the British Parliament and a man of renowned scholarship. Gilbert West was a barrister (lawyer). These two brilliant men decided that they would study the resurrection of Christ and the conversion of the apostle Paul, in the belief that they could disprove these two bulwarks of Christian faith. So they separated and spent a year in research and then came back together to share their findings. Both of these men were convinced against their own prejudices that Jesus was indeed the resurrected Lord of glory and that Paul had a true and sincere conversion that alone could account for his sudden transformation.

Frank Morrison, another lawyer, wrote a book entitled *Who Moved The Stone*. Simon Greenleaf, a professor at Harvard and Jewish by faith, wrote a book entitled *The Testimony of the Evangelist*. These books were written by men who had begun as enemies and opponents of the Christian faith. But because they considered the evidence for the Christian faith, they came to believe that the Bible was true and that Jesus was indeed the Son of God who was raised from the dead.

In John 3:16 Jesus Christ begins with the statement, '*For God...*' To understand Christianity, one must begin here. We believe there is one God who is revealed to us in three persons, the Father, the Son and the Holy Spirit. We do not believe in three Gods, but rather in one God who reveals himself as three persons. This is the great mystery of the Trinity. To reject the doctrine of the Trinity is to reject the historic Christian faith. The great twentieth-century preacher Dr Martyn Lloyd-Jones said, 'The doctrine of the Trinity is the differentiating doctrine of the Christian faith.'[11]

The nature of God

*'For God **so loved the world,** that he gave his only begotten Son,
that whosoever believeth in him should not perish,
but have everlasting life.'*

Jesus continues and says, 'For God *so loved the world...*' This
statement tells us about the attributes of God. God is a God of
love. Literally this verse reads, 'God loved the world, so much
so...' The *Westminster Confession of Faith* asks the question,
'What is God?' The answer is, 'God is a Spirit, infinite, eternal,
and unchangeable in his being, wisdom, power, holiness,
justice, goodness, and truth.'[12] Attributes are anything that are
true of God. A. W. Tozer, a famous American minister, once
wrote, 'An attribute of God is whatever God has in any way
revealed as being true of Himself.'[13]

There are *communicable attributes* of God. These are
attributes or things that are true of God, but may also be true of
man (in a relative sense) such as God's love, patience, kindness,
grace, mercy, holiness and justice. Men may be loving, patient,
kind, gracious, merciful, holy and just, but men are not perfect
in these respects. These attributes are only found in men in a
limited way. We will now consider some of the communicable
attributes that we find in God.

1. **God's love.** This is often called the most central attribute
of God. 'Swiss theologian Karl Barth was asked by a student
during a seminar in the United States, "Dr. Barth, what is the
most profound thing you have ever learned in your study of

theology?" Barth thought for a moment and then replied, "Jesus loves me, this I know, for the Bible tells me so."'[14] God's love is divided into two categories. First, there is his electing love, which is bestowed on those he has chosen. And then there is his general love. This is a love that is bestowed on the entire human race. While God's electing or saving love is reserved for those that are a part of God's eternal purposes, his general love is showered upon the entire world.

2. **God's holiness**. When we speak of the God of the Bible, we think of him in terms of his holiness and love more than any other attributes. This is not to take away from those other attributes. The holiness of God has been defined in this way: 'Holiness is the attribute of God which Scripture emphasizes more than any other. It touches every other attribute. Thus, God's justice is a holy justice, His love is a holy love, His wrath a holy wrath… Holiness implies two things: complete freedom from all moral evil, and absolute moral perfection. This is our God. He is holy. Holiness is the very beauty of God.'[15]

3. **God's patience**. The patience of God is an expression of his mercy and grace. When we speak of the patience of God, we are referring to the fact that God is longsuffering with us as his creatures. In Romans 15:5 the apostle Paul describes God as 'the God of patience'. The psalmist reminds us of God's patience in Psalm 103:8-14: 'The LORD is merciful and gracious, slow to anger, and plenteous in mercy. He will not always chide: neither will he keep his anger for ever. He hath not dealt with us after our sins; nor rewarded us according to our iniquities. For as the heaven is high above the earth, so great is his mercy toward them that fear him. As far as the east is from the west, so far hath he removed our transgressions from us. Like as a father pitieth his children, so the LORD pitieth them that fear him. For he knoweth our frame; he remembereth that we are dust.'

4. **God's grace**. Grace has often been defined by Christians as the unmerited favor of God given to those who deserve the very opposite. The grace of God is proclaimed to us in the gospel of Jesus Christ. This wonderful verse of John 3:16 is really about the grace of God. God is telling all of us that if we repent and believe on the name of his only begotten Son, he will forgive us and give unto us eternal life. This is a gracious gift and offer from God. This gift is a manifestation of God's grace. I am a great lover of the old hymns of the faith. Perhaps considering one of the greatest hymns of all times, 'Amazing Grace', will help us to understand this attribute of God.

Amazing grace

Amazing grace! How sweet the sound –
That saved a wretch like me;
I once was lost but now am found,
was blind but now I see.

Tis grace that taught my heart to fear,
and grace my fears relieved;
How precious did that grace appear
the hour I first believed.

The Lord has promised good to me,
His word my hope secures;
He will my shield and portion be
as long as life endures.

Thru many dangers toils and snares,
I have already come;
'Tis grace hath brought me safe thus far,
and grace will lead me home.

> *Yes, when this flesh and heart shall fail,*
> *and mortal life shall cease,*
> *I shall possess within the veil*
> *a life of joy and peace.*
>
> John Newton

5. God's mercy. We read in the Psalms, 'O give thanks unto the LORD; for he is good: for his mercy endureth for ever' (136:1). God's mercy comes to us out of his goodness and grace. We should also remember that God gives mercy based on his sovereign right to do so. This means God is not obligated to give mercy to anyone. He may choose to bestow mercy on us, and he may choose to withhold it. Paul the apostle writes in Romans 9:15: 'For he saith to Moses, I will have mercy on whom I will have mercy, and I will have compassion on whom I will have compassion.'

6. God's sovereignty. By sovereignty, I mean the absolute control by God over every detail of life. Someone described God's sovereignty in this way: 'This means the absolute rule and authority of God over his creation. It is a rule that governs everything without exception — creation, animals, weather, and man's salvation. God is sovereign because he is God, and because he is supreme. The God of Scripture is no fairy-tale king, but the sovereign Lord, the king of Kings (Job 23:13; I Chronicles 29:11-12; II Chronicles 20:6).'[16]

If there is one single event that could occur outside the sovereign control and will of God, then could we really trust or worship such a God? The sovereignty of God simply means that God is in control of every area of life.

a. *He is sovereign over people.* Ezra 1:1-2: 'Now in the first year of Cyrus king of Persia, that the word of the LORD by the mouth of Jeremiah might be fulfilled, the LORD stirred up the spirit of Cyrus king of Persia, that he made a proclamation throughout all his kingdom, and put it also in writing, saying, Thus saith Cyrus king of Persia, The LORD God of heaven hath given me all the kingdoms of the earth...'

b. *He is sovereign over the nations.* 'This matter is by the decree of the watchers, and the demand by the word of the holy ones: to the intent that the living may know that the most High ruleth in the kingdom of men, and giveth it to whomsoever he will, and setteth up over it the basest of men'; 'And all the inhabitants of the earth are reputed as nothing: and he doeth according to his will in the army of heaven, and among the inhabitants of the earth: and none can stay his hand, or say unto him, What doest thou?' (Daniel 4:17, 35).

c. *He is sovereign over nature.* 'He sends it forth under the whole heaven, his lightning to the ends of the earth' (Job 37:3, NKJV). 'For he says to the snow, "Fall on the earth"; likewise to the gentle rain and the heavy rain of his strength' (37:6, NKJV). 'By the breath of God ice is given, and the broad waters are frozen. Also with moisture he saturates the thick clouds; he scatters his bright clouds. And they swirl about, being turned by his guidance, that they may do whatever he commands them on the face of the whole earth. He causes it to come, whether for correction, or for his land, or for mercy' (37:10-13, NKJV). 'That you may be sons of your Father in heaven; for he makes his sun rise on the evil and on the good, and sends rain on the just and on the unjust' (Matthew 5:45, NKJV).

d. *He is sovereign over the plan of salvation.* 'And we know that all things work together for good to them that love God, to them who are the called according to his purpose. For whom he did foreknow, he also did predestinate to be conformed to the image of his Son, that he might be the firstborn among many brethren. Moreover whom he did predestinate, them he also called: and whom he called, them he also justified; and whom he justified, them he also glorified' (Romans 8:28-30).

From this passage in Romans 8 we see that God has done a whole series of things for us.

- *God foreknew us.* (This means to love before time. Foreknowledge has to do with God choosing us and loving us with a special love.)
- *God predestined us* to be conformed into the image of his Son Jesus Christ. (God wasn't taking any chances with us. He makes sure that we will become like his Son.)
- *God called us.* (This means that his Spirit convinced us of our need of Christ and drew us to the Savior's side.) 'No one can come to me unless the Father who sent me draws him; and I will raise him up at the last day' (John 6:44, NKJV).
- *God justified us.* (Knowing that we could never produce a holiness or righteousness of our own that would satisfy his law, God forgave us and dressed us in the righteousness of Christ alone.)
- *God glorified us*. (This means that although we are still alive, God has insured that our future glorification in heaven is certain. By joining us to Christ, we are as good as glorified already!)

7. **God's justice**. The justice of God is inflexible. Divine justice makes it necessary for God to punish all sin and every sinner. Although God's justice demands the punishment of the sinner, it may also accept the vicarious sacrifice of another. This is seen in the fact that God the Father is willing to forgive repentant sinners based on the sacrificial death of his Son. Christ died in the place of all those the Father had chosen and had given to him. Therefore, when a person comes to faith in Christ, God

can forgive them of their sins because he has already punished those sins in his only Son, the Lord Jesus Christ. Here are some of the verses in the Bible that speak of the justice of God.

- *Romans 6:23*: 'For the wages of sin is death; but the gift of God is eternal life through Jesus Christ our Lord.'
- *Hebrews 9:27*: 'And as it is appointed unto men once to die, but after this the judgment.'
- *Ezekiel 18:4*: 'Behold, all souls are mine; as the soul of the father, so also the soul of the son is mine: the soul that sinneth, it shall die.'

Now we turn to the *incommunicable attributes* of God. These are things that can only be true of God, such as God's omniscience, omnipresence and omnipotence.

1. **God's omniscience**. This simply means that God knows all things. He knows our thoughts before we think them. He knows what we will do tomorrow. There is nothing in word, thought or deed that can be hidden from the Lord. One theologian described God's omniscience this way: 'By the omniscience of God we mean that He knows Himself and all other things ... whether they be past, present, or future, and that He knows them perfectly and from all eternity. He knows things immediately, simultaneously, exhaustively and truly.'[17] God knows all things, for he is omniscient.

Author and theologian R. C. Sproul made this statement about God's omniscience: 'The word *omniscience* means "to have all (*omni*) knowledge (science)". It is a term that is properly applied to God alone. Only a being that is infinite and eternal is capable of knowing everything. The knowledge of a finite creature is always limited by a finite being. God, being infinite, is able to be aware of all things, to understand all things, and to comprehend all things. He never learns anything or acquires new knowledge. The future as well as the past and present are completely known to him. He is surprised by nothing.'[18]

2. **God's omnipresence**. This means that God is everywhere at the same time. The psalmist said in Psalm 139:7-12: 'Whither shall I go from thy spirit? or whither shall I flee from thy presence? If I ascend up into heaven, thou art there: if I make my bed in hell, behold, thou art there. If I take the wings of the morning, and dwell in the uttermost parts of the sea; even there shall thy hand lead me, and thy right hand shall hold me. If I say, Surely the darkness shall cover me; even the night shall be light about me. Yea, the darkness hideth not from thee; but the night shineth as the day: the darkness and the light are both alike to thee.'

3. **God's omnipotence**. The omnipotence of God simply means that God is all powerful. God can do anything that he wills or chooses to do. But since God cannot sin, we say that he can only do those things that are consistent with his holy nature. God cannot look upon sin. This means God cannot tolerate sin or excuse it. Sin must be punished. This is why John 3:16 is so important and precious to us. And God cannot lie, he cannot deny himself or fail to keep his promises that he gives to us in his Word.

Once when Jesus was asleep in a boat that was crossing the Sea of Galilee during a terrible storm, the disciples woke him up out of fear. Jesus rebuked both the men and the storm. He said, 'O ye, of little faith.' The response of the disciples to his miracle of calming the storm was to say to one another, 'What manner of man is this, that even the winds and the sea obey him!' (Matthew 8:27). On another occasion, Jesus came to his disciples during a storm by walking on the water. His astonished disciples cried out that they thought they saw a ghost. 'It is a spirit!' The word 'spirit' in the Greek New Testament was *phantasma* and is the same word from which we get our English word phantom. Peter even got out of the boat and tried to walk to Jesus. Both of these incidents happened on the Sea of Galilee. And both of these incidents caused the disciples of Jesus to question his identity. 'Who is this man, that even the winds and the sea obey him?'

1. Do we know who Jesus is? It is only through the Son of God that we can discover who the Father is and what he is like.
2. There is nothing more important than knowing who Jesus is.
3. A famous essay entitled 'The Incomparable Christ' captures the essence of the person and work of Jesus Christ.

The Incomparable Christ

More than nineteen hundred years ago there was a Man born contrary to the laws of life. This man lived in poverty and was reared in obscurity. He did not travel extensively. Only once did He cross the boundary of the country in which He lived; that was during His exile in childhood. He possessed neither wealth nor influence. His relatives were inconspicuous and had neither training nor formal education. In infancy He startled a king; in childhood He puzzled doctors; in manhood He ruled the course of nature, walked upon the billows as if pavements, and hushed the sea to sleep. He healed the multitudes without medicine and made no charge for His service. He never wrote a book, yet all the libraries of the country could not hold the books that have been written about Him. He never wrote a song, and yet he has furnished the theme for more songs than all the songwriters combined. He never founded a college, yet all the schools put together cannot boast of having as many students. He never marshaled an army, nor drafted a soldier, nor fired a gun; and yet no leader ever had more volunteers who have, under His authority, made more rebels stack arms and surrender

*without a shot fired. He never practiced psychiatry, and yet He
has healed more broken hearts than all the doctors far and near.
Every seventh day the wheels of commerce cease their turning
and multitudes wend their way to worshiping assemblies to
pay homage and respect to Him. The names of the past proud
statesmen of Greece and Rome have come and gone. The names
of the past scientists, philosophers, and theologians have come
and gone, but the name of this Man abounds more and more.
Though time has spread nineteen hundred years between the
people of this generation and the scene of His crucifixion, yet
He still lives. Herod could not destroy Him and the grave could
not hold Him. He stands forth upon the highest pinnacle of
heavenly glory, proclaimed of God, acknowledged by angels,
adored by saints, and feared by demons, as the living, and risen
Son of God, our Lord and our Savior Jesus Christ.*

Author unknown

Bishop Phillips-Brooks (author of the Christmas carol 'O Little
Town of Bethlehem'), when referring to the impact that the
solitary life of Jesus has had on history, wrote:

*Nineteen wide centuries have come
and gone (since the time of Christ).
Today, He is the centerpiece of the
human race and the
leader of the column of progress.
I am far within the mark when I
say that all the armies that ever marched,
all the navies that have ever sailed,
all the parliaments that have ever sat,
and all the Kings that ever reigned,
put together, have not affected the life of man upon
this earth as powerfully
as has ... THAT ONE SOLITARY LIFE.*

The gift of God

*'For God so loved the world, **that he gave his only begotten Son**, that whosoever believeth in him should not perish, but have everlasting life.'*

Jesus continued and said, '*...that he gave his only begotten Son*'. God gave us his Son as a gift to each of us. What exactly does this mean? In eternity past, the triune God met in a council with the three persons of the Godhead and made a covenant. A covenant is an agreement between two or more people. In this covenant, the Father agreed to choose a certain number of people to give to his Son. This is seen in several verses. In Ephesians 1:4 we read: 'According as he hath chosen us in him before the foundation of the world, that we should be holy and without blame before him in love.' And in John 6:37 Jesus said, 'All that the Father giveth me shall come to me; and him that cometh to me I will in no wise cast out.' The Son agreed to come and live their life and die their death. In John 1:14 we are told: 'And the Word was made flesh, and dwelt among us, (and we beheld his glory, the glory as of the only begotten of the Father,) full of grace and truth.' And the Holy Spirit agreed to draw these people to Christ. Jesus said, 'No man can come to me, except the Father which hath sent me draw him: and I will raise him up at the last day' (John 6:44).

The meaning of this gift in John 3:16 is explained for us in Romans 8:32: 'He that spared not his only Son, but delivered him up for us all, how shall he not with him freely give us

all things?' What does it mean that the Father spared not his
own Son but delivered him up for us all? The word 'delivered'
simply means that the Father turned Jesus over to the cross and
all of its horrors and agonies.

1. Jesus was delivered up to the shame of the cross.
2. Jesus was delivered up to the reproach of the cross.
3. Jesus was delivered up to the suffering of the cross.

Jesus lived and died as our substitute. Jesus lived the life
we could not live. Jesus lived for thirty-three years on this
earth and during that time he never sinned. Every time he kept
the law and obeyed his Father, he was doing that for all of
those who would believe on him. In a sense, Jesus was saying
to his Father, 'Consider my obedience the obedience of all
those that you chose and gave to me.' Jesus died the death
we should have died. By going to the cross, Jesus took all of
the guilt and shame of our sins and became responsible for
them. The punishment that should have been poured out on
us was poured out on him instead. Isaiah 1:18 reads: 'Come
now, let us reason together, saith the LORD: though your sins be
as scarlet, they shall be as white as snow; though they be red
like crimson, they shall be as wool.' I am told that if you look
at something that is red through a red lens, it will appear white.
So it is, that when God looks at our red sins through the blood
of Christ, our sins are as white as snow.

Jesus himself is the speaker who gives us this wonderful
verse of John 3:16. It is amazing that Jesus says, 'For God so
loved the world, that he gave his only begotten Son...' If Jesus
did not believe that he was God, this verse would make no
sense at all. In fact, if Jesus were just a mere man, his words
in this verse would be outrageously arrogant. It would be
like me saying, 'For God so loved the world, that he gave *me*
that whosoever believeth on *me* should not perish but have

everlasting life.' John 3:16 only makes sense if Jesus is truly God.

British scholar C. S. Lewis understood this. He knew that if Jesus was not God, he was either a liar or a lunatick. Thus, we have three different options open to us concerning the real identity of Jesus Christ. Jesus is either the Lord of the universe as he said he was, or he was a liar, or a lunatick. These are the only three options available to us concerning the question 'Who is Jesus Christ?' C. S. Lewis writes:

> *A man who was merely a man and said the sort of things Jesus said would not be a great moral teacher. He would either be a lunatic — on a level with the man who says he is a poached egg — or else he would be the Devil of Hell. You must make your choice. Either this man was, and is, the Son of God: or else a madman or something worse. You can shut Him up for a fool, you can spit at Him and kill Him as a Demon; or you can fall at His feet and call Him Lord and God. But let us not come with any patronizing nonsense about His being a great human teacher. He has not left that open to us. He did not intend to.[19]*

Jesus is the gift the Father gave to us in order that we might have eternal life and the forgiveness of sins. The historic Christian faith defends the view that Jesus was not merely a man; it also believes that Jesus is the eternal Son of God. How can we demonstrate that Jesus is not just a man but is also the very God who created the universe and who is to be worshipped, obeyed, loved and followed? There are a number of things that set Jesus apart from all other religious leaders and point to his deity:

1. His sinless life;
2. His miracles;
3. His wisdom and the authority of his teaching;

4. His fulfilment of the Messianic prophecies in the Old Testament;
5. His resurrection from death and the grave.

What do we conclude about a man who lived such a life that no one could ever point out even one sin; who had the ability to work the most amazing miracles that many people were eyewitness to; who had greater wisdom than any other man before him and who taught with such authority that even his enemies were astonished; who just happened to fulfil all 333 Messianic prophecies contained in the Old Testament; and who not only predicted his death and resurrection but came forth from the grave and was seen alive by many hundreds of people? The only logical conclusion that we can draw from such a man and from such a life is that this man was truly God in the flesh.

The promise of God

'For God so loved the world, that he gave his only begotten Son,
that whosoever believeth in him should not perish, but have
everlasting life.'

Jesus finished the verse in John 3:16 by adding this wonderful
and amazing promise, *'that whosoever believeth in him should
not perish but have everlasting life'*. This verse promises that
whoever *repents* and *believes* on his Son will not perish but
will be given the gift of eternal life. Faith means that you
believe that Jesus is God, that he died for your sins, and that he
was raised from the dead. 'That if thou shalt confess with thy
mouth the Lord Jesus, and shalt believe in thine heart that God
hath raised him from the dead, thou shalt be saved' (Romans
10:9). Repentance means to turn from sin.

A good example of repentance is found in an interesting
story that came out of the archives of an old West Texas town.
Many years ago, there was an account of a minister who
went into the jail to preach the gospel to the prisoners inside.
It was a dark and stormy night. Lightning was crashing and
the lamps were dim. In that old jail, the minister preached the
wonderful gospel story of Jesus Christ. Those prisoners that
night fell on their faces and accepted Christ as their Savior. A
newspaper writer had gone along to help the old minister. He
witnessed this remarkable sight and recorded it in poetic verse
for his paper. Many years later, another minister was thumbing
through the archives of that little town and came across this
amazing story.

The ninety men in the marshal's den

*I'm going to preach, and I'm going to teach, to the ninety men
in here, (in the midst of a violent storm raging outside). Of
the words of love, from the throne above, and his words rang
out loud and clear. I'll preach for you of a Savior true, and
a happy home on high. Where the angels dwell, where all are
saved from Hell, and where the righteous never die. And he said
a prayer in the prison there, as the ninety bowed their heads,
to the old Choctaw and the Chickasaw, to the whites and the
blacks and the reds. He prayed for the chief in his unbelief, and
the dark highwayman bold, to the robber crew and the bandits
too, to the criminals young and old. Then he sang a hymn in
the prison grim, he sang, 'Turn sinner, turn.' 'It's not too late
to reach God's gate ere the lamp holds out to burn.' And then
from his bed, from the black and the red, a broken outlaw too.
With trembling steps to the parson crept, and he shivered as all
in the cold. And a bitter flash, as the lightning's crashed, showed
his features pale and stern, as he bowed his head he solemnly
said, 'Dear God, I am resolved to turn.' And it seemed to me I
shall never see, a scene so great so grand, as the white and the
red and their darkened friends around that Christian one did
stand. While the light came down, like a silver crown, for the
promise came to all. For the ninety men in the marshal's den
heard only the Savior's call. And a bitter flash, as the lightning's
crashed, showed their features pale and stern. As they all bowed
their heads they all solemnly said, 'Dear God, we are resolved
to turn.'*

Author unknown

That is repentance, my dear friends. It is turning from sin.
Repentance and faith alike are the gifts of God. God graciously
gives these gifts to his elect, and they are enabled to put their
faith in him. Repentance was taught by Jesus in Luke 13:3:

'I tell you, Nay: but, except ye repent, ye shall all likewise perish.' And by Peter in Acts 2:38: 'Then Peter said unto them, Repent…'

Repentance is turning from sin with a deep and godly sorrow that we have sinned against God and against his laws. Are you willing to turn from your sins? Are you willing to turn from breaking the laws of God? The laws of God are made plain in the Scriptures. The Ten Commandments give us a concise summary of those laws.

The Ten Commandments
(a summary from Exodus 20:1-17)

1. Thou shalt have no other gods before me.
2. Thou shalt not make unto thee any graven image.
3. Thou shalt not take the name of the LORD thy God in vain.
4. Thou shalt remember the Sabbath day, to keep it holy.
5. Thou shalt honour thy father and thy mother.
6. Thou shalt not kill.
7. Thou shalt not commit adultery.
8. Thou shalt not steal.
9. Thou shalt not lie.
10. Thou shalt not covet.

We have all broken the laws of God. Because of this, we are under the wrath of God. Romans 3:10 says, 'As it is written, There is none righteous, no, not one.' In Romans 3:23 we read, 'For all have sinned, and come short of the glory of God.' And finally, in Romans 6:23 Paul the apostle says, 'For the wages of sin is death; but the gift of God is eternal life through Jesus Christ our Lord.'

Faith, like repentance, is a gift from God. We read in Ephesians 2:8-9: 'For by grace are ye saved through faith; and that not of yourselves: it is the gift of God: not of works, lest

any man should boast.' To become a Christian, a person needs
to repent and turn from their sins and put their faith and trust in
the Lord Jesus Christ. The promise in this verse is that whoever
does this will be forgiven and will be given the gift of eternal
life. In John 6:37, Jesus gave his disciples another promise
when he said, 'All that the Father giveth me shall come to me;
and him that cometh to me I will in no wise cast out.'

Conclusion

We have considered the four great truths that John 3:16 teaches us. To summarize them once again they were:

1. The existence of God
2. The nature of God
3. The gift of God
4. The promise of God.

It is my desire that all who will read this will also put their trust in the Lord Jesus Christ. You might be asking, 'What must I do?' It is very simple. Cry out to God with this brief prayer found in Luke 18:13: 'O God be merciful to me a sinner.' Romans 10:9 is so clear: 'That if thou shalt confess with thy mouth the Lord Jesus Christ, and believe in thine heart that God hath raised him from the dead, thou shalt be saved.'

My personal testimony of faith in Christ

Here is my personal story of how I came to faith in Jesus Christ. Many years ago in a locker room at a track meet in Saginaw, Michigan, I was gambling with some friends while waiting for my event to take place. Out of nowhere, it seemed, a discussion arose that caused several of us who were gambling to wonder whether it was right or wrong to do so. We decided to ask another athlete who was there that night what he thought about this question. This young man was a dedicated Christian. He was also one of the top sprinters and hurdlers in the United States at that time. He was undefeated in his event (the 120 yard high hurdles and the 180 yard low hurdles).

That evening while I was gambling with my team mates, this young man was on the other side of the locker room lying on a bench. At the very moment I was gambling, he was praying that he might have an opportunity to win somebody to Christ that night. He even prayed that he would rather have an opportunity to speak to someone about Christ than win his track events that evening. While he was praying in this way, I was across the locker room gambling with my friends. What I did not know was that God was going to answer his prayers that night.

Out of nowhere the discussion arose that caused me and one other athlete to go over and ask this fellow athlete if it was right or wrong to gamble. The reason we decided to ask him was because of his testimony that he was a Christian. He was living a life that was so different from any of ours. He did not swear, steal, lie, and do the kinds of things that so many of us did. These things did not make him a Christian, but they were evidence that something about him was very different. So I, and another friend, went over and asked him if the Bible said anything about gambling.

What I remember so vividly about that night was that my friend did not really deal with our initial question. He simply told us that the main issue before a holy God was not gambling but rather whether or not we knew the Lord Jesus Christ. After we asked him this question about gambling, he reached down and inside his racing spikes he had stuffed a little New Testament. He pulled out this copy of the Word of God and began to tell us about the Lord Jesus Christ. He told us the very things that I have outlined here in this booklet on 'Authentic Christianity 101'. He told me that Jesus was the Son of God, that the Father sent Christ into the world to live in my place and to satisfy the law of God so that his righteousness could be given to me as a gift. He also told me that Jesus died on the cross for all those the Father had chosen. Jesus, he said, had paid the debt in full that we owe to God. He also made it clear that after the death of Jesus Christ, he was buried, and that on the Sunday he was raised from the dead. Then he told me that I needed to repent of my sin and put my faith in Jesus Christ as the only way of being forgiven and having eternal life. He quoted John 14:6 where Jesus said, '...I am the way, the truth, and the life: no man cometh unto the Father, but by me.'

That evening in that locker room in Saginaw, Michigan, the God of the universe that I had never known came down and took hold of my life. He gave me life, and with that new life, he gave me the ability to repent and believe. I was changed, not by my own power or strength, but by the mighty and sovereign power of God.

What happened to me in that locker room is what I desire for each of you who may read this. Charles Wesley wrote a famous hymn, a stanza of which vividly portrays what happens when a person becomes a Christian:

> *Long my imprisoned spirit lay,*
> *Fast bound by sin and nature's night,*
> *Thine eye diffused a quickening ray,*
> *I woke, the dungeon flamed with light.*
> *My chains fell off, my heart was free,*
> *I rose went forth and followed Thee.*

That evening in a locker room, I became a Christian. God came to me and found me and gave me eternal life. But this gift of salvation came as he enabled me to repent and to believe.

What you must do now

Do you believe in God? Do you believe that you are a sinner and that you have broken God's laws and deserve to be punished for your sins? Do you realize that you cannot save yourself? Do you realize that salvation only comes through faith in Jesus Christ? Do you believe that Jesus died on the cross for your sins and that he rose again from the dead? Do you believe that Jesus is alive right now and that he is the only way to heaven?

If you believe these things, then I invite you to pray with me here. Right now, ask God for forgiveness. Acknowledge that Jesus is the Son of God. Pray that you might be given the ability to repent and believe. Jesus said, 'Come unto me, all ye that labor and are heavy laden, and I will give you rest' (Matthew 11:28). O, my dear friend, come to Jesus today. Right now, come to him in faith and repentance. Cry out to him, and he will not turn you away. Here is a suggested prayer that you can pray to God.

The sinner's prayer

'O God in heaven, be merciful to me a sinner. I believe that Jesus Christ is your only Son and that he died on the cross for my sins. I believe that he was buried and that he rose again from the dead. I confess that I am a sinner and that I need to be forgiven of all my sins. Help me to repent and to turn from my sins. Give me faith to believe and to trust Christ who alone can give me salvation. Father in heaven I accept Jesus Christ as my Lord and Savior. I desire above all else to love and serve him all the days of my life. This I ask in the name of Jesus, Amen.'

When a person becomes a Christian, he or she should do the following things:

1. Obey the Lord by being baptized and make a profession of faith at a local Bible-believing church.
2. Begin to read your Bible daily.
3. Find a church where you can worship God on a weekly basis. (Make sure that church believes that the Bible is the inspired and infallible Word of God, and preaches the gospel of Jesus Christ.)
4. Read good Christian books that will help you to grow in the knowledge and grace of God and of his Son Jesus Christ.
5. Find other Christians to fellowship with. This can be done by attending a good Bible-believing church. The person who gave you this booklet can help you find others who share the same faith that has been outlined here.

This is 'Authentic Christianity 101'. This is the message that Jesus gave us in John 3:16. In this most well-known verse in the Bible, we have the very basics of the Christian message.

For God so loved the world, that he gave his only begotten Son, that whosoever believeth in him should not perish, but have everlasting life.

What a wonderful message to proclaim. What a wonderful message to accept and to rest in today. My dear friend, are you resting in this great message today?

If you would like to read more about this topic of 'Authentic Christianity 101', I would recommend the following books:

1. *Knowing God* by J. I. Packer
2. *The Pursuit of God* by A. W. Tozer
3. *The Sermon on the Mount* by Dr Martyn Lloyd-Jones
4. *Nothing But The Truth* by John MacArthur
5. *Ashamed of the Gospel* by John MacArthur
6. *What the Bible Teaches About Worship* by Robert L. Dickie
7. *Be Sure What You Believe* by Joe Nesom.

Notes

1. *The Shorter Catechism*, Question 4, What is God? (Published by Banner of Truth Trust), p.1.

2. William Evans, *The Great Doctrines of the Bible* (Moody Press, Chicago, 1966), p.16.

3. Norman Geisler, interview by Nancy Pearcey, in 'Geisler's Rebuttal: An Appeal to Common Sense', *Bible-Science Newsletter*, March 1985.

4. D. James Kennedy, *Why I Believe* (Word Publishing,1980), p.16.

5. Dr Hugh Ross, quoted from the web site: *Fulfilled Prophecy: Evidence for the Reliability of the Bible,* http://www.reasons.org/resources/apologetics/prophecy.shtml.

6. John Ankerberg & John Weldon, *The Facts On Why You Can Believe The Bible* (Harvest House Publishers, 2004), p.28.

7. Ankerberg & Weldon, *The Facts On Why You Can Believe The Bible* (Harvest House Publishers, 2004), p.8.

8. Mark Eastman, Chuck Missler, *The Creator Beyond Time And Space* (Costa Mesa, Ca: The Word For Today, 1996), p.87.

9. T. J. McCrossan, *The Bible: Its Christ and Modernism* (The Christian Alliance Publishing Company, 1925), p.56.

10. Os Guinness, *The Long Journey Home* (Zondervan Press, 2001), p.13.

11. Dr Martyn Lloyd-Jones, quoted by John Blanchard in *The Complete Gathered Gold* (Evangelical Press, 2006), p.257.

12. *The Westminster Confession of Faith* (The Publication Committee of the Free Presbyterian Church of Scotland, 1976), pp.287-8.

13. A. W. Tozer, quoted by Peter Jeffery in *The Christian Handbook* (Bryntirion Press, printed by Evangelical Press of Wales, 2000), pp.126-7.

14. Karl Barth, quoted by R. C. Sproul in *Essential Truths in the Christian Faith* (Tyndale House Publishers, 1992), p.31.

15. Peter Jeffery, *The Christian Handbook* (Bryntirion Press, printed by Evangelical Press of Wales, 2000), p.127.

16. Jeffery, *The Christian Handbook*, p.127.

17. Henry Clarence Thiessen, *Introductory Lectures in Systematic Theology* (Eerdmans Publishing Company, 1968), p.124.

18. R. C. Sproul, *Essential Truths of the Christian Faith* (Tyndale House Publishers, 1992), p.45.

19. C. S. Lewis, *Mere Christianity* (New York: Macmillan Publishing Co. Inc.,1952), p.56.

Scripture index

	Page		Page
Old Testament		Matthew 11:28	44
Genesis 1:1	6, 19	Matthew 21:23	12
Genesis 1:9	19	Luke 13:3	38-9
Genesis 2:7	19	Luke 18:13	41
Exodus 20:1-17	39	John 1:1-4	6
Numbers 24:17	16	John 1:14	7, 33
1 Chronicles 29:11-12	26	John 3:16	5, 6, 7, 8, 22, 23,
2 Chronicles 20:6	26		25, 30, 33, 34-5, 37, 41, 45
Ezra 1:1-2	26-7	John 6:37	33, 40
Job 23:13	26	John 6:44	28, 33
Job 26:7	19	John 14:6	43
Job 37:3, 6, 10-13	27	Acts 2:38	39
Psalm 14:1	8	Romans 1:19-20	8
Psalm 103:8-14	24	Romans 3:10	39
Psalm 136:1	26	Romans 3:23	39
Psalm 139:7-12	30	Romans 6:23	29, 39
Isaiah 1:18	34	Romans 8:28-30	28
Ezekiel 14:14	19	Romans 8:32	33-4
Ezekiel 18:4	29	Romans 9:15	26
Daniel 4:17, 35	27	Romans 10:9	37, 41
		Romans 15:5	24
New Testament		Ephesians 1:4	33
Matthew 5:45	27	Ephesians 2:8-9	39-40
Matthew 7:12	20	Hebrews 9:27	29
Matthew 8:27	30	2 Timothy 3:16-17	14

Pages 15-17 also list twenty-six Messianic prophecies of the Old Testament with twenty-six references to where they are fulfilled in the New Testament.